The Cyber Rat Chronicles: A Journey into Ethical Hacking

the educational nature of the content. Ethical hacking is a serious and legitimate field with established ethical guidelines and legal frameworks. This book seeks to inspire interest and understanding in the subject matter while maintaining a commitment to responsible and ethical storytelling.

We hope you enjoy this educational journey into the realms of ethical hacking, where the boundaries of imagination meet the principles of cybersecurity.

Akash Gupta

Author

CONTENTS:

Chapter 1

Whisker Warriors - Introduction to Rat Ethical Hacking

In the dimly lit corners of the digital realm, a new breed of warriors emerges—ones with whiskers and an insatiable appetite for securing cyberspace. Welcome to the world of "Whisker Warriors," where the unconventional meets the ethical, and rats take center stage in the battle against cyber threats.

Unveiling the Whiskered Operatives

The opening chapter of "The Cyber Rat Chronicles" sets the stage by introducing readers to the curious world of rat ethical hacking. Imagine a clandestine network where rodents, armed with a keen sense of curiosity and an innate ability to navigate mazes, become the unsung heroes of cybersecurity.

Rat ethical hacking, a term that may sound whimsical at first, delves into the realm of utilizing these intelligent creatures to identify vulnerabilities in digital systems. In this introductory chapter, readers are invited to shed preconceived notions and open their minds to the unexplored potential of rodent intelligence in the realm of technology.

The Genesis of Rodent Involvement

The chapter begins with a historical exploration, tracing the roots of rodent involvement in human affairs. From ancient civilizations using rats to carry messages across battle lines to the emergence of cyber threats in the 21st century, the narrative weaves a tale of interconnectedness between rats and human endeavors.

Rat ethical hacking, however, is not a whimsical idea born out of fantasy. It finds its roots in the need for innovative and unconventional approaches to cybersecurity. As traditional methods prove insufficient against evolving threats, the stage is set for a new kind of warrior—one with fur, four legs, and an uncanny ability to squeeze through the tightest digital loopholes.

Unconventional Allies: Humans and Rats

The chapter highlights the unique partnership between humans and rats in the pursuit of ethical hacking.

Drawing parallels between the agility of rats in physical mazes and the complexity of digital ones, readers begin to see the symbiotic relationship forming. Ethical hackers, with their technical expertise, guide and collaborate with their whiskered allies to navigate the intricate paths of cyberspace.

The introduction also emphasizes the ethical considerations underpinning this unconventional collaboration. The rats, far from being exploited, become willing participants in a mission to protect digital landscapes. The chapter elucidates on the careful selection, training, and well-being of these rodent operatives, ensuring their comfort and security in their cyber endeavors.

Whisker Warriors' Toolkit

As readers delve deeper into the first chapter, they are introduced to the unique toolkit of the Whisker Warriors. Forget about conventional hacking devices; here, it's all about whiskers, sharp instincts, and an uncanny ability to detect anomalies. The narrative provides an engaging exploration of the rat's sensory prowess, highlighting how their acute senses make them ideal candidates for identifying digital irregularities.

Moreover, the chapter discusses the incorporation of technology into the rats' arsenal. Tiny sensors and communication devices, designed with the utmost consideration for the rodents' well-being, enable seamless interaction between the whisker warriors and their human counterparts.

The Call to Adventure

As the introductory chapter nears its conclusion, readers are left with a sense of anticipation and curiosity. The call to adventure echoes in the digital air as the stage is set for a journey into uncharted territory. The Whisker Warriors, armed with their unique skill set, stand poised to confront the challenges of the digital frontier.

The chapter closes with an invitation to readers—a call to embrace the unconventional, to question established norms, and to embark on a journey alongside these unlikely heroes. The world of rat ethical hacking beckons, promising not just an exploration of cybersecurity but a redefinition of the very essence of ethical hacking.

In "Whisker Warriors: Introduction to Rat Ethical Hacking," readers take their first steps into a world where the line between fiction and reality blurs, and where the whiskered operatives of cyberspace await their moment to shine.

Chapter 2

Cheese and Codes - Understanding the Basics of Rat Security

In the clandestine world of rat ethical hacking, where whiskers meet wires, the journey begins with a fundamental understanding of the connection between cheese and codes. "Cheese and Codes" serves as the gateway to comprehending the basic principles that underpin the unique approach of rat security in the digital landscape.

The Cheese-Analogy: Unveiling Digital Assets

The chapter kicks off by drawing a clever analogy between the irresistible allure of cheese for a rat and the valuable digital assets that attract cyber threats. In the realm of cybersecurity, data is the modern-day cheese, coveted by hackers who navigate the intricate mazes of the internet in search of vulnerabilities.

Readers are guided through the digital maze, where the scent of information attracts both benevolent defenders and malicious intruders. The cheese-analogy becomes a lens through which the essential concepts of digital security are presented, making the complexities of the cyber landscape accessible to both novices and seasoned cybersecurity enthusiasts.

Rat Security 101: Protecting the Cheese

As the chapter unfolds, the focus shifts to Rat Security 101—an essential primer on safeguarding the digital cheese. Just as a rat might employ strategic routes and vigilance to protect its prized morsel, the principles of rat security involve proactive measures to defend against cyber threats.

Topics such as encryption, authentication, and access control are explored in a rat-centric context, emphasizing the need for robust defenses to ensure the safety of valuable digital assets. The chapter serves as a bridge between conventional cybersecurity practices and the innovative strategies employed by the Whisker Warriors.

Whiskered Intricacies: Navigating Digital Mazes

An intriguing aspect of "Cheese and Codes" is the exploration of the intricate paths that rats navigate both in physical mazes and in the vast expanse of cyberspace. The chapter dives into the parallels between the rodent's ability to adapt to changing mazes and the dynamic nature of cybersecurity challenges.

Readers gain insights into the agility of the Whisker Warriors as they traverse the digital labyrinth, employing a combination of instinct and training. The narrative weaves a tale of resilience and adaptability, underscoring the importance of embracing change in the face of evolving cyber threats.

The Digital Cheeseboard: Identifying Vulnerabilities

A significant portion of the chapter is dedicated to unraveling the concept of the digital cheeseboard—a metaphorical space where rats and ethical hackers collaborate to identify vulnerabilities. Readers are introduced to the tools and techniques employed by the Whisker Warriors to conduct thorough assessments of digital landscapes.

From penetration testing to vulnerability scanning, the chapter sheds light on the methodologies that bridge the gap between traditional cybersecurity practices and the innovative, rat-centric approach. The narrative emphasizes the symbiotic relationship between the human ethical hacker and their whiskered ally, working together to fortify the defenses of digital cheese.

The Cheddar Principle: Layers of Defense

A highlight of "Cheese and Codes" is the introduction of the Cheddar Principle—a layered approach to defense that mimics the protective layers surrounding a block of cheese. Readers are guided through the concept of defense in depth, where multiple layers of security measures act in concert to thwart potential cyber threats.

From firewalls and antivirus software to intrusion detection systems, the chapter unravels the layers of the Cheddar Principle. Each layer serves as a bulwark against different types of cyber-attacks, reinforcing the notion that a holistic approach is essential in safeguarding digital assets.

Ethical Cheese Tasting: Assessing Risk

The chapter concludes with an exploration of ethical cheese tasting—an intriguing concept that involves assessing the risk associated with different types of digital cheese. Readers are introduced to risk management strategies that allow organizations to make informed decisions about the value and importance of their digital assets.

Through scenarios and case studies, the narrative illustrates how ethical hackers, in collaboration with their rat counterparts, conduct risk assessments to prioritize defenses and allocate resources effectively. The chapter leaves readers with a newfound appreciation for the nuanced art of balancing risk and reward in the dynamic landscape of cybersecurity.

In "Cheese and Codes: Understanding the Basics of Rat Security," readers embark on a journey through the fundamentals of rat ethical hacking. From the symbolism of cheese to the intricacies of digital mazes, the chapter lays the groundwork for a deeper exploration of the innovative strategies that define the Whisker Warriors' approach to cybersecurity.

Chapter 3

Furry Footprints - Tracing Rodent Activity in Cyberspace

In the enthralling realm of rat ethical hacking, understanding the subtle traces left behind by whiskered operatives is paramount. "Furry Footprints" takes readers on a captivating journey, delving into the art and science of tracing rodent activity in the vast expanse of cyberspace.

The Intricate Dance: Rodents in Cyberspace

The chapter unfolds with an exploration of the intricate dance between rats and cyberspace. Readers are introduced to the concept of "Furry Footprints" as a metaphorical representation of the traces left by rodents while navigating the digital terrain. Much like footprints in the sand, these markers become essential clues for ethical hackers seeking to understand and analyze rodent activity.

The narrative emphasizes the agility of the Whisker Warriors, their ability to move stealthily through the vast cyber-mazes, leaving behind a trail of digital footprints. This dance is not one of intrusion but rather a carefully orchestrated ballet of detection, where the rats play a central role in revealing vulnerabilities within the digital landscape.

Whiskered Forensics: Unraveling the Digital Clues

A significant portion of the chapter is dedicated to exploring the world of whiskered forensics—an emerging field that combines traditional digital forensics with the unique insights provided by rat ethical hacking. Readers are guided through the process of unraveling digital clues left by the whisker warriors, from analyzing log files to deciphering patterns in network traffic.

Whiskered forensics becomes a powerful tool in the ethical hacker's arsenal, allowing them to reconstruct the sequence of events and understand the tactics employed by potential adversaries. The narrative weaves a tale of collaboration between human analysts and their rodent counterparts, highlighting the complementary nature of their skills in the pursuit of cyber resilience.

Tailored Analytics: Data from the Digital Tails

As readers delve deeper into "Furry Footprints," the concept of tailored analytics takes center stage. Much like a rat's tail, which provides balance and stability, the digital tails left behind by rodent activity offer valuable insights into the cybersecurity landscape. The chapter explores how ethical hackers harness these digital tails to tailor their analytics, creating a nuanced understanding of the threats faced.

From behavioral analysis to anomaly detection, readers are introduced to the sophisticated techniques used by ethical hackers to make sense of the digital tails. The narrative underscores the importance of context, emphasizing that each tail tells a unique story that contributes to the larger narrative of cybersecurity.

Rodent Artistry: Mapping Whiskered Journeys

An artistic element emerges in "Furry Footprints" as readers are introduced to the concept of rodent artistry—the creation of maps that depict the intricate journeys of Whisker Warriors through the cyber-mazes. These maps, a fusion of data visualization and creativity, become invaluable tools for ethical hackers seeking to understand the dynamics of rodent activity.

The chapter takes a detour into the world of cybercartography, exploring how these maps provide a visual representation of the digital landscape as experienced by the rats. Readers gain insights into the strategic placement of virtual cheese (digital assets) and the various routes taken by the rodents, offering a unique perspective that goes beyond traditional cybersecurity analytics.

The Whispering Trail: Communication among Whisker Warriors

A fascinating aspect of "Furry Footprints" is the exploration of the whispering trail—an intricate network of communication among Whisker Warriors. Much like a whispered secret passed among allies, the rats exchange information through subtle cues and shared experiences in cyberspace.

Readers gain an understanding of the nuances of rat communication and how ethical hackers leverage this unique form of interaction. The narrative unfolds as a tale of collaboration, where the whispering trail becomes a conduit for sharing insights, warnings, and discoveries among the whiskered operatives.

Ethical Tracking: Balancing Surveillance and Privacy

The chapter concludes with an exploration of ethical tracking—a delicate balance between surveillance and privacy in the realm of rat ethical hacking. Readers are prompted to ponder the ethical considerations surrounding the tracing of rodent activity, acknowledging the need for responsible and respectful practices in this unconventional field.

The narrative navigates the complexities of ethical tracking, emphasizing the importance of transparency and consent. It becomes evident that while Furry Footprints offer valuable insights, the ethical hacker's responsibility extends to ensuring the well-being and privacy of the whiskered operatives involved.

In "Furry Footprints: Tracing Rodent Activity in Cyberspace," readers embark on a journey through the fascinating world of rat ethical hacking. From the intricate dance of rodents in cyberspace to the artistry of mapping their journeys, the chapter unfolds as a captivating exploration of the digital footprints that pave the way for a more secure and resilient cyber landscape.

Chapter 4

Cryptic Nests - Creating a Secure Environment for Ethical Rats

As the digital realm intertwines with the world of rat ethical hacking, the concept of "Cryptic Nests" emerges as a pivotal chapter in understanding the importance of providing a secure environment for the whiskered operatives. This chapter delves into the intricacies of safeguarding the habitats where the Whisker Warriors dwell, ensuring not only their physical well-being but also the integrity of their cyber exploits.

The Sanctity of the Nest

"Cryptic Nests" opens with a reflection on the sanctity of the nest, the haven where Whisker Warriors retreat after their cyber expeditions. The narrative weaves an image of safety and security, drawing parallels between the physical nests of rodents and the virtual sanctuaries where ethical hacking operations are planned and executed.

Readers are invited to envision the digital nests as more than mere spaces; they are the command centers where ethical hackers and their whiskered allies collaborate. The chapter unfolds as a testament to the symbiotic relationship between these unconventional partners, emphasizing the need for secure havens in the dynamic landscape of cybersecurity.

Digital Architectures: Building Rat-Resilient Spaces

The narrative transitions into the exploration of digital architectures designed with rat resilience in mind. The creation of secure spaces involves meticulous planning, taking inspiration from the intricate construction of rodent nests in the natural world.

Readers gain insights into the principles of digital architecture, where the emphasis is on creating environments that accommodate the unique needs of the Whisker Warriors. From secure communication channels to encrypted databases, the chapter navigates the elements that fortify these digital nests against external threats.

Cybersecurity Infrastructure: A Home for Whisker Warriors

An integral part of "Cryptic Nests" revolves around the cybersecurity infrastructure that forms the foundation of the secure environments for ethical rats. Readers are introduced to advanced technologies and protocols, such as intrusion detection systems and network segmentation, that safeguard the digital habitats from potential adversaries.

The narrative emphasizes the proactive measures taken to ensure the resilience of these nests. It becomes clear that cybersecurity infrastructure isn't just a technical necessity; it is the digital fortress that protects the whiskered operatives as they embark on their cyber journeys.

Rodent-Proofing: Securing Physical and Virtual Boundaries

A significant portion of the chapter is dedicated to the concept of rodent-proofing—securing both physical and virtual boundaries to prevent unauthorized access. Much like a physical nest requires protection from external predators, the digital nests of Whisker Warriors demand robust defenses to thwart potential cyber threats.

Readers explore the innovative methods employed to secure these boundaries, from biometric access controls to AI-driven threat detection. The narrative weaves a tale of vigilance and adaptability, mirroring the dynamic nature of both rodent behavior and the evolving landscape of cybersecurity threats.

Whisker-Friendly Technologies: Enhancing Rat Well-Being

The well-being of Whisker Warriors is a focal point in "Cryptic Nests," prompting an exploration of whisker-friendly technologies. Ethical hackers collaborate with experts in animal behavior and welfare to design technologies that not only enhance security but also prioritize the comfort and health of the rodent operatives.

From ergonomic interfaces for rat-friendly communication to ambient environmental controls within the digital nests, readers gain insights into the harmonious integration of technology and animal welfare. The chapter underscores the ethical considerations that underscore this unconventional collaboration, ensuring that the well-being of the Whisker Warriors remains paramount.

Training Grounds: Simulating Real-World Cyber Scenarios

The chapter unfolds further as readers are introduced to the training grounds—simulated environments where Whisker Warriors hone their skills in confronting real-world cyber scenarios. These virtual spaces serve as crucibles for ethical hacking exercises, allowing the rats to practice and refine their cyber techniques in a controlled and secure environment.

The narrative delves into the intricacies of training programs, from gamified simulations to real-time feedback mechanisms. It becomes evident that the preparation of Whisker Warriors extends beyond theoretical knowledge, emphasizing the practical skills needed to navigate the complexities of cyberspace.

Ethical Considerations: Balancing Innovation and Compassion

As "Cryptic Nests" draws to a close, readers are prompted to reflect on the ethical considerations surrounding the creation of secure environments for ethical rats. Balancing innovation with compassion becomes a central theme, as the narrative explores the responsibilities that come with integrating animals into the world of technology.

The chapter invites readers to contemplate the delicate equilibrium between pushing the boundaries of innovation and maintaining a deep sense of empathy for the Whisker Warriors. It becomes evident that the creation of cryptic nests is not merely a technical endeavor but a moral obligation to ensure the ethical treatment of the rodent operatives.

Beyond Boundaries: The Future of Cryptic Nests

The concluding section of the chapter offers a glimpse into the future of cryptic nests. Readers are invited to envision a world where secure environments for ethical rats become standard practice in the realm of cybersecurity. The narrative speculates on the evolution of technology and ethical considerations, anticipating a future where the boundaries between the physical and digital worlds seamlessly blend to create sanctuaries for both humans and rats alike.

In "Cryptic Nests: Creating a Secure Environment for Ethical Rats," readers embark on a journey through the foundational principles that uphold the unconventional collaboration between humans and rodents in the field of ethical hacking. From the sanctity of the nest to the innovative technologies that secure digital boundaries, the chapter serves as a testament to the harmonious integration of ethics, technology, and animal welfare.

Chapter 5

Byte-sized Espionage - Techniques of the Cyber Rat

In the clandestine world where whiskers meet wires, "Byte-sized Espionage" unfolds as a pivotal chapter, revealing the intricacies of the techniques employed by Cyber Rats. This segment of "The Cyber Rat Chronicles" takes readers on a thrilling journey through the digital landscape, exploring the unique espionage methods that make the Whisker Warriors a formidable force in the realm of ethical hacking.

The Whiskered Arsenal

The chapter commences with an exploration of the whiskered arsenal—the unique tools and abilities that set Cyber Rats apart in the world of ethical hacking. Much like a spy's toolkit, the whiskered arsenal encompasses a range of skills, from the innate curiosity and agility of rats to the sophisticated technologies integrated into their cyber exploits.

Readers are introduced to the concept of "Byte-sized Espionage" as a fusion of traditional espionage techniques and cutting-edge technology. The narrative sets the stage for an exploration of how these byte-sized operatives navigate the vast cyber-maze to uncover vulnerabilities.

Infiltration Techniques: Navigating the Digital Maze

The essence of Cyber Rat espionage lies in their infiltration techniques, and the chapter takes a deep dive into the strategies employed by the Whisker Warriors. Analogous to a rat maneuvering through physical mazes, these rodents traverse the digital labyrinth, guided by a combination of instinct and training.

The narrative unfolds as a tale of adaptability and resourcefulness, exploring how Cyber Rats exploit vulnerabilities in software, networks, and systems. Readers gain insights into the art of silent infiltration, where the whiskered operatives leave minimal traces while uncovering potential threats and weaknesses.

Tailored Reconnaissance: Gathering Digital Intel

A significant portion of the chapter is dedicated to the concept of tailored reconnaissance—a process through which Cyber Rats gather digital intelligence to inform their ethical hacking endeavors. Readers are introduced to the nuanced methods employed in gathering information, from eavesdropping on network traffic to sniffing out potential vulnerabilities.

Much like a spy tailing a target, Cyber Rats employ their keen senses to identify weak points in the digital infrastructure. The narrative explores the collaboration between rats and human ethical hackers in customizing reconnaissance strategies, tailoring their approaches to the specific challenges posed by diverse cyber landscapes.

Covert Communication: Whispering in Binary

A fascinating aspect of "Byte-sized Espionage" is the exploration of covert communication techniques among Cyber Rats. The chapter delves into the intricacies of whispering in binary—an unconventional form of communication where rodents and ethical hackers exchange information through subtle digital cues.

Readers are invited to envision a world where Cyber Rats, equipped with tiny communication devices, engage in a silent dialogue with their human counterparts. The narrative unfolds as a dance of encrypted messages, emphasizing the seamless integration of rodent instincts with the sophistication of modern cybersecurity communication.

Social Engineering: The Rat's Gambit

As the chapter progresses, readers are introduced to the concept of social engineering—the Rat's Gambit. Much like a masterful gambit in a game of chess, Cyber Rats employ social engineering techniques to manipulate human behavior and gain access to sensitive information.

The narrative navigates through scenarios where rats use their charm, agility, and, at times, the power of cuteness to persuade humans to unwittingly reveal valuable information. The Rat's Gambit becomes a strategic element in the cyber espionage playbook, showcasing the synergy between rodent instincts and human psychology.

Furry Phreaks: Mastering the Art of Cyber Intrusion

A highlight of "Byte-sized Espionage" is the exploration of Furry Phreaks—Cyber Rats who specialize in mastering the art of cyber intrusion. The chapter unveils the advanced techniques employed by these elite operatives, from bypassing security measures to exploiting zero-day vulnerabilities.

Readers gain insights into the dynamic world of cyber intrusions, where Furry Phreaks operate as digital acrobats, navigating the most challenging cyber landscapes. The narrative emphasizes the balance between innovation and responsibility, showcasing how these whiskered operatives push the boundaries of ethical hacking while adhering to a code of conduct.

Squeaky Safeguards: Ethical Boundaries in Cyber Espionage

The chapter concludes with an exploration of Squeaky Safeguards—ethical boundaries that guide Cyber Rats in their espionage endeavors. Readers are prompted to contemplate the delicate equilibrium between pushing the limits of innovation and maintaining a strong ethical foundation.

The narrative underscores the responsibility borne by ethical hackers, both human and rodent, in navigating the fine line between espionage and intrusion. It becomes evident that Byte-sized Espionage isn't just about technological prowess but about upholding a moral compass in the pursuit of cyber resilience.

The Future of Whiskered Espionage

As the chapter draws to a close, readers are offered a glimpse into the future of whiskered espionage. The narrative speculates on the evolving landscape of ethical hacking, envisioning a world where Cyber Rats continue to play a vital role in pushing the boundaries of innovation while upholding the principles of responsible and ethical hacking.

In "Byte-sized Espionage: Techniques of the Cyber Rat," readers embark on a captivating exploration of the unique espionage methods that define the Whisker Warriors. From infiltration techniques to covert communication, the chapter unveils the byte-sized world where rodents and humans collaborate in the quest for a secure digital frontier.

Chapter 6

Rodent Reconnaissance - Gathering Intel with Whiskered Operatives

In the clandestine world of rat ethical hacking, where the scent of information permeates the digital air, "Rodent Reconnaissance" stands as a pivotal chapter, unraveling the intricacies of how Whisker Warriors engage in the art of gathering intelligence. This segment of "The Cyber Rat Chronicles" delves into the methodologies and strategies employed by these whiskered operatives as they navigate the vast cyber-mazes in pursuit of valuable information.

The Instinctive Detectives

The chapter unfolds with a tribute to the innate detective skills of the Whisker Warriors. Much like natural detectives exploring crime scenes, these rodents possess an uncanny ability to sniff out digital clues. The narrative paints a vivid picture of rats weaving through the labyrinth of cyberspace, relying on their heightened senses to detect anomalies and potential threats.

Readers are introduced to the concept of Rodent Reconnaissance as an amalgamation of instinctive detection and purposeful exploration. The narrative sets the stage for understanding how these rodent detectives become essential assets in uncovering the secrets hidden within the digital terrain.

Cyber-Sniffing: Detecting Digital Anomalies

A significant aspect of the chapter is dedicated to the art of cyber-sniffing—a technique where Whisker Warriors leverage their acute sense of smell to detect digital anomalies. Readers are guided through scenarios where rats, equipped with specially designed sensors, navigate through digital landscapes, identifying unusual patterns and potential security breaches.

The narrative emphasizes the synergy between natural instincts and technological augmentation, showcasing how cyber-sniffing becomes a powerful tool in the rat's repertoire. These whiskered detectives serve as the first line of defense, detecting anomalies that may elude traditional cybersecurity measures.

Tailoring Reconnaissance Strategies

As the chapter progresses, readers are invited into the world of tailoring reconnaissance strategies—a process where ethical hackers collaborate with their whiskered counterparts to customize approaches based on the unique challenges posed by different cyber landscapes. Each scenario requires a tailored strategy, reflecting the dynamic nature of the digital frontier.

The narrative explores the partnership between humans and rats in devising reconnaissance plans that consider factors such as the type of information sought, the architecture of the digital maze, and potential adversaries. This tailoring process becomes a testament to the adaptability and intelligence of the Whisker Warriors.

The Maze Mapping Initiative

A captivating element of "Rodent Reconnaissance" is the introduction of the Maze Mapping Initiative—a collaborative effort to create detailed maps of the cyber-mazes. Readers are immersed in the process as rats equipped with miniature cameras and sensors traverse the digital terrain, documenting the layout and potential vulnerabilities.

The narrative unfolds as a tale of exploration and discovery, with the maze maps becoming invaluable assets for ethical hackers. The intricate pathways, virtual cheese locations (representing digital assets), and potential danger zones are meticulously documented, providing a blueprint for strategic cybersecurity measures.

Collaborative Data Analysis: Decrypting Rodent Intel

The chapter takes a deeper dive into the collaborative data analysis phase, where human ethical hackers decrypt the intelligence gathered by the Whisker Warriors. Much like code-breaking in the realm of espionage, this process involves deciphering the data gathered by the rodents, transforming it into actionable insights.

Readers gain insights into the synergy between rodent instincts and human analytical skills. The narrative explores the challenges and triumphs of decrypting rodent intel, emphasizing the collaborative nature of this unconventional approach to cybersecurity.

A.I.-Enhanced Reconnaissance: The Tech-Rat Synergy

The narrative unfolds further as readers are introduced to the concept of A.I.-enhanced reconnaissance—a fusion of rodent instincts and artificial intelligence. Whisker Warriors, equipped with advanced sensors and communication devices, collaborate with AI systems to enhance their ability to detect and analyze digital anomalies.

The chapter navigates through scenarios where the synergy between natural instincts and technological augmentation elevates the reconnaissance capabilities of the Whisker Warriors. This tech-rat synergy becomes a testament to the innovative approach embraced in the realm of rodent reconnaissance.

Whiskered Intel in Action: Real-world Scenarios

A significant portion of "Rodent Reconnaissance" is dedicated to exploring real-world scenarios where whiskered intel is put into action. Readers are immersed in case studies and examples illustrating how the information gathered by the Whisker Warriors contributes to the identification and mitigation of cyber threats.

The narrative unfolds as a series of digital adventures, where the instincts of the rodent detectives prove instrumental in uncovering vulnerabilities, identifying malicious activities, and fortifying cyber defenses. The real-world impact of rodent reconnaissance becomes evident as the Whisker Warriors play a crucial role in safeguarding digital landscapes.

Ethical Considerations: The Rat's Right to Privacy

As the chapter draws to a close, readers are prompted to ponder the ethical considerations surrounding rodent reconnaissance. The narrative navigates through the delicate balance between harnessing the unique skills of Whisker Warriors and respecting their right to privacy.

It becomes evident that ethical hackers, in their pursuit of cybersecurity, are guardians not only of digital landscapes but also of the well-being and ethical treatment of their rodent allies. The chapter serves as a reflection on the responsibility that comes with integrating animals into the realm of technology and espionage.

The Future of Rodent Reconnaissance

The concluding section of the chapter offers a glimpse into the future of rodent reconnaissance. Readers are invited to envision a world where the collaboration between humans and rats evolves, pushing the boundaries of innovation and ethical hacking. The narrative speculates on the continued integration of rodent intelligence in cybersecurity efforts, anticipating a future where Whisker Warriors continue to play a vital role in the digital landscape.

In "Rodent Reconnaissance: Gathering Intel with Whiskered Operatives," readers embark on a captivating journey through the unconventional world of ethical hacking, where rodents become indispensable allies in the quest for cyber resilience. From instinctive detection to collaborative data analysis, the chapter unfolds as a testament to the symbiotic relationship between human ingenuity and the unique skills of the Whisker Warriors.

Chapter 7

Squeaky Safeguards - Protecting Against Unethical Intrusions

In the dynamic realm of rat ethical hacking, where whiskers and wires converge, "Squeaky Safeguards" emerges as a pivotal chapter. This segment of "The Cyber Rat Chronicles" delves into the critical role of safeguarding against unethical intrusions, exploring the measures and principles implemented to ensure the integrity of rodent-led cybersecurity efforts.

The Ethical Imperative

The chapter unfolds by establishing the ethical imperative that underpins the entire rodent ethical hacking initiative. Readers are reminded of the responsibility that ethical hackers, both human and rodent, bear in safeguarding digital landscapes while adhering to a strict code of ethics.

"Squeaky Safeguards" becomes a testament to the commitment to integrity and ethical conduct, emphasizing that the pursuit of cybersecurity must be conducted with the highest moral standards. The narrative sets the stage for understanding the multifaceted safeguards in place to prevent unethical intrusions.

The Rodent Code of Conduct

Central to the theme of "Squeaky Safeguards" is the exploration of the Rodent Code of Conduct—a set of guidelines and principles that govern the behavior of Whisker Warriors. Readers are introduced to the fundamental tenets that guide rodent ethical hacking, ensuring that their activities align with ethical standards.

The narrative unfolds as a journey through the principles of transparency, consent, and responsible use of technology. The Rodent Code of Conduct becomes a foundation for building trust between humans and rodents, laying the groundwork for a collaborative and ethical approach to cyber security.

Informed Consent: The Whiskered Agreement

A significant portion of the chapter is dedicated to the concept of informed consent—a critical component of the Whiskered Agreement. Readers are immersed in the process where rodent operatives are provided with information about their roles, tasks, and potential risks involved in ethical hacking.

The narrative navigates through the nuances of communication between humans and rodents, emphasizing the importance of ensuring that the whiskered operatives participate willingly and are aware of the nature of their missions. Informed consent becomes a cornerstone in establishing a relationship based on trust and respect.

Whisker-Friendly Technologies

The chapter delves into the implementation of whisker-friendly technologies—a proactive approach to ensuring the well-being of Whisker Warriors engaged in ethical hacking activities. Readers gain insights into the development of technologies that not only enhance security measures but also prioritize the comfort and health of the rodent operatives.

From ergonomic communication interfaces to ambient environmental controls within the digital nests, the narrative paints a picture of a harmonious integration of technology and animal welfare. Whisker-friendly technologies exemplify the commitment to safeguarding the physical and mental well-being of the rodent allies.

Digital Boundaries: Respecting Rodent Privacy

Respecting rodent privacy emerges as a key theme in "Squeaky Safeguards." The narrative navigates through the establishment of digital boundaries, ensuring that the cyber activities of Whisker Warriors are conducted in a manner that respects their right to privacy.

Readers are prompted to contemplate the delicate balance between leveraging rodent intelligence for ethical hacking and respecting the individual autonomy of the whiskered operatives. The establishment of digital boundaries becomes a reflection of the commitment to ethical conduct in the realm of rodent ethical hacking.

Oversight and Governance

An integral part of "Squeaky Safeguards" revolves around the implementation of oversight and governance mechanisms. Readers are introduced to the structures and processes in place to monitor and regulate rodent ethical hacking activities, ensuring compliance with ethical standards and legal frameworks.

The narrative explores the role of oversight committees, comprising both human and rodent representatives, in reviewing and approving missions. Governance becomes a safeguard against potential ethical breaches, creating a system of checks and balances that upholds the integrity of rodent-led cybersecurity efforts.

Continuous Training and Evaluation

The chapter emphasizes the importance of continuous training and evaluation in maintaining the ethical standards of Whisker Warriors. Readers are immersed in the world of ongoing education for both human and rodent operatives, ensuring that they stay abreast of the latest cybersecurity developments and ethical considerations.

The narrative unfolds as a journey through training programs, simulations, and skill assessments. Continuous training becomes a proactive measure to fortify the ethical foundation of rodent ethical hacking, fostering a culture of learning and adaptability.

Ethical Dilemmas: Navigating Gray Areas

As "Squeaky Safeguards" progresses, readers are confronted with the exploration of ethical dilemmas—challenges that arise in the gray areas of rodent ethical hacking. The narrative navigates through scenarios where ethical considerations may be ambiguous, prompting ethical hackers to make thoughtful and principled decisions.

Readers are prompted to reflect on the complexities inherent in the intersection of technology, ethics, and animal welfare. The chapter becomes a platform for contemplating the ethical dilemmas faced by both human and rodent ethical hackers, highlighting the need for ethical reflection and decision-making.

Whiskered Advocacy: Raising Awareness

The chapter concludes with an exploration of whiskered advocacy—an initiative to raise awareness about rodent ethical hacking and its ethical considerations. Readers are immersed in the efforts to communicate the principles of ethical conduct, transparency, and respect for animal rights within the cybersecurity community and the broader public.

The narrative unfolds as a call to action, encouraging readers to become advocates for ethical hacking practices that prioritize both human and rodent welfare. Whiskered advocacy becomes a tool for fostering a culture of ethical responsibility and awareness in the evolving landscape of cybersecurity.

The Future of Squeaky Safeguards

The concluding section of the chapter offers a glimpse into the future of Squeaky Safeguards. Readers are invited to envision a world where the ethical principles and safeguards implemented in rodent ethical hacking serve as a model for responsible and transparent cybersecurity practices.

The narrative speculates on the continued evolution of safeguards, anticipating advancements in technology and ethical frameworks that further enhance the integrity of rod

Chapter 8

Cheese Diplomacy - Building Alliances in the Cyber Landscape

In the intricate dance of whiskers and wires, "Cheese Diplomacy" emerges as a pivotal chapter in "The Cyber Rat Chronicles." This segment delves into the art of building alliances in the cyber landscape, exploring the unique role of Whisker Warriors in fostering collaborations that transcend species boundaries. As the digital world becomes increasingly interconnected, this chapter unravels the strategies and dynamics of Cheese Diplomacy, where rats and humans forge partnerships to navigate the complex web of cybersecurity.

The Whiskered Ambassadors

The chapter unfolds with an exploration of Whisker Warriors as ambassadors in the digital realm. Much like diplomats representing their nations, these rodents become ambassadors of a unique kind, fostering alliances between the animal kingdom and the world of ethical hacking.

Readers are introduced to the concept of Cheese Diplomacy as a symbolic bridge connecting the instincts of rodents with the intellectual prowess of ethical hackers. The narrative sets the stage for understanding how these whiskered ambassadors play a crucial role in building alliances for the greater good of cybersecurity.

Cyber Diplomacy 101

A significant portion of the chapter is dedicated to Cyber Diplomacy 101—an exploration of the principles that govern alliances in the digital landscape. Readers are immersed in the dynamics of collaboration between human ethical hackers, organizations, and the Whisker Warriors.

The narrative navigates through the nuances of trust-building, communication strategies, and the establishment of common goals. Cyber Diplomacy becomes a guide for forging alliances that go beyond traditional boundaries, fostering a sense of unity in the shared mission of securing the cyber landscape.

Rodent-Human Collaboration Models

As the chapter progresses, readers are introduced to various models of rodent-human collaboration in the cyber landscape. From collaborative research projects to joint cybersecurity initiatives, the narrative explores the multifaceted nature of alliances between humans and rats.

The storytelling unfolds as a tapestry of partnerships, where the unique strengths of each species complement the other. These collaboration models serve as blueprints for fostering synergy in the pursuit of innovative and effective cybersecurity solutions.

Cheese Summits: Convening for Cybersecurity

A captivating element of "Cheese Diplomacy" is the concept of Cheese Summits—gatherings where humans and Whisker Warriors convene to discuss and strategize cybersecurity efforts. The narrative paints a vivid picture of these diplomatic engagements, where rodents and humans sit side by side to exchange insights, share discoveries, and plan future initiatives.

Readers are immersed in the collaborative atmosphere of Cheese Summits, where the boundaries between species blur, and a shared commitment to cybersecurity takes center stage. The narrative becomes a celebration of diversity and collaboration, emphasizing the power of unity in the face of cyber threats.

Cross-Species Communication

A significant focus of the chapter is on the exploration of cross-species communication—a unique aspect of Cheese Diplomacy. The narrative delves into the innovative ways in which humans and rodents communicate in the cyber landscape, transcending linguistic and cultural differences.

From specially designed communication interfaces to the incorporation of rodent-friendly technologies, readers gain insights into the efforts to bridge the communication gap. The chapter becomes a testament to the adaptability and creativity required in establishing effective cross-species collaborations.

Cultural Exchange: Embracing Diversity

The narrative unfolds further as readers are introduced to the concept of cultural exchange in the world of Cheese Diplomacy. Ethical hackers and Whisker

Warriors engage in a form of cultural exchange, where they learn from each other's unique perspectives, approaches, and problem-solving strategies.

The storytelling navigates through scenarios where the blending of human and rodent cultures leads to the emergence of innovative cybersecurity methodologies. Cultural exchange becomes a catalyst for growth and mutual understanding, enriching the collaborative landscape of Cheese Diplomacy.

Whiskered Ambassadors in Action: Case Studies

As "Cheese Diplomacy" progresses, readers are immersed in real-world case studies that showcase the impact of whiskered ambassadors in action. The narrative unfolds as a series of success stories where rat-human alliances lead to breakthroughs in cybersecurity, from the identification of novel threats to the development of innovative defense strategies.

Each case study becomes a testament to the effectiveness of Cheese Diplomacy in addressing the dynamic challenges of the cyber landscape. These stories of collaboration serve as inspiration for the continued exploration of alliances between species.

Cybersecurity Aid Programs

An integral part of the chapter revolves around the exploration of cybersecurity aid programs—a form of Cheese Diplomacy where ethical hackers extend their expertise to support rodent communities in need. Readers are introduced to initiatives where humans collaborate with Whisker Warriors to strengthen the cybersecurity resilience of rodent populations.

The narrative navigates through the implementation of aid programs, from educational campaigns on cybersecurity hygiene for rodents to the provision of advanced technologies for enhanced security. Cybersecurity aid becomes a cornerstone of Cheese Diplomacy, fostering a sense of global responsibility in the quest for a secure cyber landscape.

Whiskered Diplomacy Beyond Borders

The chapter concludes with an exploration of Whiskered Diplomacy beyond borders. Readers are invited to envision a future where Cheese Diplomacy transcends geographical and species boundaries, leading to global collaborations in the name of cybersecurity.

The narrative speculates on the potential for a united front against cyber threats, where humans and Whisker Warriors from diverse regions work together seamlessly. Whiskered Diplomacy becomes a beacon of hope in the evolving landscape of cybersecurity

Chapter 9

The Whisker Code - Ethical Guidelines for Rodent Hacktivism

In the labyrinth of ethical hacking, where whiskers meet wires, "The Whisker Code" emerges as a guiding light, illuminating the path of rodent hacktivism. This chapter in "The Cyber Rat Chronicles" delves into the principles and ethical guidelines that govern the activities of Whisker Warriors as they navigate the complex world of cybersecurity. As rodent hacktivism becomes an integral part of the ethical hacking landscape, "The Whisker Code" stands as a testament to the commitment to responsible and principled conduct in the pursuit of a secure digital frontier.

The Moral Compass of Whisker Warriors

The chapter unfolds by establishing the moral compass that guides the actions of Whisker Warriors. Readers are immersed in the ethos of rodent hacktivism, where the well-being of both rodents and the digital landscape takes precedence. The Whisker Code becomes a symbolic representation of the ethical principles that govern these unconventional operatives.

The narrative sets the stage for an exploration of how ethical guidelines serve as a foundation for building trust and credibility in the world of rodent hacktivism. Whisker Warriors are portrayed not only as skilled operatives but as guardians of a higher purpose – the ethical pursuit of cyber security.

Transparency and Openness

At the heart of "The Whisker Code" lies the principle of transparency and openness. The narrative navigates through the commitment to clear communication and disclosure, emphasizing the importance of Whisker Warriors openly sharing their intentions, methodologies, and findings with human ethical hackers.

Readers are invited to envision a collaborative environment where transparency becomes a cornerstone of trust. The narrative unfolds as a reflection on how open communication fosters understanding and cooperation between species, ensuring that the objectives of rodent hacktivism align with ethical standards.

The Right to Digital Privacy

A significant portion of the chapter is dedicated to exploring the right to digital privacy—a principle upheld by Whisker Warriors in their ethical endeavors. The narrative delves into how rodent hacktivism is conducted with a deep respect for the privacy rights of individuals in the digital landscape.

Readers are prompted to contemplate the delicate balance between cybersecurity objectives and the protection of individual liberties. The Whisker Code becomes a safeguard against unwarranted intrusions, emphasizing the responsibility of Whisker Warriors to respect the digital privacy of entities within the cyber realm.

Non-Discrimination and Inclusivity

The Whisker Code champions the principles of non-discrimination and inclusivity. The narrative unfolds as a celebration of diversity, reflecting the commitment to equality in rodent hacktivism. Whisker Warriors operate without bias, considering all entities in the cyber landscape, regardless of their origin, with impartiality.

Readers are immersed in a narrative that underscores how the principles of non-discrimination and inclusivity contribute to a fair and ethical approach in rodent hacktivism. The Whisker Code becomes a beacon of equity in the pursuit of a secure digital ecosystem.

Cybersecurity for the Greater Good

The narrative progresses into the exploration of the principle of cybersecurity for the greater good. Whisker Warriors, guided by the Whisker Code, are portrayed as ethical hackers with a sense of responsibility to protect not just individual entities but the entire cyber landscape.

Readers gain insights into how rodent hacktivism aligns with a broader mission of securing the digital realm for the benefit of all. The narrative unfolds as a testament to the collective responsibility shared by Whisker Warriors in their commitment to the greater good.

Preservation of Rodent Welfare

A central theme in "The Whisker Code" revolves around the preservation of rodent welfare. The narrative navigates through the ethical considerations that Whisker Warriors prioritize to ensure the well-being of their rodent counterparts engaged in hacktivism.

From providing comfortable and secure digital nests to incorporating whisker-friendly technologies, readers are immersed in a narrative that underscores the commitment to rodent welfare as an integral part of ethical hacking endeavors. The Whisker Code becomes a guide for ethical hackers to prioritize the physical and mental health of their rodent allies.

Continuous Education and Adaptability

As the chapter progresses, readers are introduced to the principles of continuous education and adaptability embedded in the Whisker Code. Ethical hackers, both human and rodent, are portrayed as lifelong learners, committed to staying abreast of evolving cybersecurity landscapes.

The narrative unfolds as a journey through ongoing training programs, simulations, and skill assessments. The Whisker Code becomes a dynamic set of guidelines, reflecting the need for continuous education and adaptability to address the ever-changing challenges of the digital frontier.

Responsible Disclosure and Collaboration

The Whisker Code places a strong emphasis on responsible disclosure and collaboration. The narrative explores the ethical considerations involved in reporting vulnerabilities and collaborating with relevant stakeholders in the cybersecurity community.

Readers are immersed in scenarios where Whisker Warriors work in tandem with human ethical hackers to responsibly disclose vulnerabilities, contributing to the development of effective countermeasures. The Whisker Code becomes a framework for building trust and fostering collaborative relationships in the pursuit of a secure cyber landscape.

Whisker Advocacy and Public Awareness

A significant focus of "The Whisker Code" revolves around whisker advocacy and public awareness. Ethical hackers are portrayed as advocates for rodent welfare and ethical hacking practices, working to raise awareness about the unique role of Whisker Warriors in the digital landscape.

Readers are prompted to envision a world where public awareness campaigns contribute to a deeper understanding of rodent hacktivism. The Whisker Code becomes a tool for not only guiding ethical conduct but also for advocating for the recognition and appreciation of the contributions made by Whisker Warriors.

Enforcement and Accountability

The chapter concludes with an exploration of the enforcement mechanisms and accountability embedded in the Whisker Code. Ethical hackers, both human and rodent, are portrayed as accountable stewards of cybersecurity, upholding the principles outlined in the Whisker Code.

Readers are immersed in scenarios where adherence to ethical guidelines is not just a recommendation but a commitment, backed by mechanisms that ensure accountability. The Whisker Code becomes a framework for building a culture of responsible conduct and accountability in the world of rodent hacktivism.

The Future of Whisker Ethics

The concluding section of the chapter offers a glimpse into the future of whisker ethics. Readers are invited to envision a world where the principles outlined in the Whisker Code serve as a foundation for the continued evolution of ethical hacking practices, shaping the ethical landscape of the digital frontier.

The narrative speculates on the potential impact of the Whisker Code in inspiring future generations of ethical hackers, fostering a culture of responsible conduct, collaboration, and respect for all entities within the cyber landscape. The Whisker Code becomes a legacy, guiding the ethical footsteps of Whisker Warriors on the path to a secure and inclusive digital future.

In "The Whisker Code: Ethical Guidelines for Rodent Hacktivism," readers embark on a journey through the ethical considerations that underpin the activities of Whisker Warriors in the realm of cybersecurity. From transparency and inclusivity to rodent welfare and responsible disclosure, the Whisker Code becomes a compass, guiding ethical hackers in their mission to secure the digital frontier with integrity and purpose.

Chapter 10

Whisker Harmony - Achieving Synergy in the Cyber Ecosystem

In the ever-evolving landscape where technology and biology converge, "Whisker Harmony" takes center stage as the culminating chapter in "The Cyber Rat Chronicles." This segment delves into the concept of achieving synergy in the cyber ecosystem, exploring the harmonious integration of Whisker Warriors and human ethical hackers. As the narrative unfolds, readers are immersed in a journey that underscores the interconnectedness of species, the fusion of natural instincts with technological prowess, and the collaborative spirit that defines the future of ethical hacking.

The Symphony of Whisker Harmony

The chapter opens with a metaphorical exploration of the symphony of Whisker Harmony. Readers are invited to envision a harmonious interplay of whiskers and wires, where the unique strengths of both rats and humans contribute to a melodious collaboration in the vast cyber ecosystem.

The narrative sets the stage for a celebration of diversity, emphasizing that true harmony arises when different elements come together to create something greater than the sum of their parts. Whisker Harmony becomes a metaphor for the symbiotic relationship between Whisker Warriors and human ethical hackers.

Convergence of Instinct and Technology

At the heart of Whisker Harmony lies the exploration of the convergence of instinct and technology. The narrative navigates through scenarios where the natural instincts of rodents, honed over centuries of evolution, seamlessly integrate with cutting-edge technologies wielded by human ethical hackers.

Readers are immersed in a tale of adaptability and innovation, where rodent intuition becomes a valuable asset in deciphering complex cyber landscapes. The narrative unfolds as a testament to the power of harmonizing the primal wisdom of nature with the ingenuity of technology in the pursuit of a secure digital ecosystem.

Whisker-Driven Innovation

A significant portion of the chapter is dedicated to showcasing whisker-driven innovation—a phenomenon where the unique skills and behaviors of Whisker Warriors inspire groundbreaking approaches in ethical hacking. The narrative explores how the agility, curiosity, and problem-solving instincts of rats catalyze innovative solutions to cybersecurity challenges.

Readers are invited to envision a world where rodent-driven innovation becomes a driving force in ethical hacking endeavors. The narrative unfolds as a celebration of unconventional ideas and approaches that emerge from the harmonious collaboration between humans and Whisker Warriors.

Dynamic Teamwork: Whiskers and Wires

As Whisker Harmony progresses, readers are introduced to the concept of dynamic teamwork—a synergy where whiskers and wires complement each other in the cyber ecosystem. The narrative delves into scenarios where Whisker Warriors and human ethical hackers form cohesive teams, each contributing their unique strengths to tackle diverse cyber challenges.

The storytelling unfolds as a reflection on the power of diversity in teams, emphasizing that the collaboration between species amplifies creativity and problem-solving capabilities. Dynamic teamwork becomes a cornerstone in achieving Whisker Harmony, fostering an environment where mutual respect and collaboration flourish.

Ecosystem Resilience and Adaptation

The narrative progresses into an exploration of ecosystem resilience and adaptation—a theme that underscores the capacity of the cyber ecosystem to withstand and adapt to emerging threats. Readers gain insights into how the harmonious collaboration between Whisker Warriors and ethical hackers contributes to the resilience of the digital landscape.

The narrative navigates through scenarios where the adaptability of rodents and the technological prowess of humans create a formidable defense against cyber threats. Ecosystem resilience becomes a testament to the strength that emerges from the harmonious integration of natural and artificial intelligence.

Whisker Harmony in Practice: Case Studies

A significant focus of the chapter revolves around real-world case studies that illustrate Whisker Harmony in practice. The narrative unfolds as a series of stories where the collaboration between Whisker Warriors and human ethical hackers leads to successful outcomes, from identifying and neutralizing threats to fortifying digital defenses.

Each case study becomes a narrative thread, weaving together the achievements and challenges faced by the harmonious collaboration between species. Readers are immersed in the practical applications of Whisker Harmony, witnessing the positive impact on the cybersecurity landscape.

Holistic Cybersecurity: The Whisker Harmony Approach

The narrative delves into the concept of holistic cybersecurity—a comprehensive approach that embraces the interconnectedness of technology, nature, and human ingenuity. Whisker Harmony becomes a guiding philosophy, emphasizing the need for ethical hackers to consider the broader ecosystem when designing and implementing cybersecurity measures.

Readers are invited to contemplate the implications of a holistic cybersecurity approach, where the integration of natural instincts with technological solutions results in a more resilient and adaptive digital ecosystem. The narrative unfolds as a call to embrace a mindset that transcends traditional boundaries and fosters a harmonious coexistence between whiskers and wires.

Ethical Considerations in Whisker Harmony

As the chapter progresses, ethical considerations come into focus in the context of Whisker Harmony. The narrative navigates through scenarios where ethical hackers, both human and rodent, grapple with dilemmas and challenges that arise from the harmonious collaboration.

Readers are prompted to reflect on the importance of upholding ethical principles, ensuring that the pursuit of cybersecurity aligns with values of transparency, privacy, and respect for all entities within the cyber ecosystem. Ethical considerations become a guiding compass, steering the course of Whisker Harmony in a responsible and principled direction.

Future Prospects of Whisker Harmony

The concluding section of the chapter offers a glimpse into the future prospects of Whisker Harmony. Readers are invited to envision a world where the collaborative efforts between Whisker Warriors and ethical hackers continue to evolve, shaping the future of ethical hacking and cybersecurity.

The narrative speculates on the potential advancements in technology, the emergence of new threats, and the innovative solutions that may arise from the ongoing integration of whiskers and wires. The future of Whisker Harmony becomes a canvas for imagination, where the collaborative spirit between species continues to be a driving force in securing the digital frontier.

In "Whisker Harmony: Achieving Synergy in the Cyber Ecosystem," readers embark on a journey that transcends traditional boundaries, celebrating the harmonious integration of Whisker Warriors and human ethical hackers. From the convergence of instinct and technology to dynamic teamwork and ecosystem resilience, the chapter becomes a testament to the transformative power of collaboration in the ever-evolving cyber landscape

www.ingramcontent.com/pod-product-compliance
Lightning Source LLC
Chambersburg PA
CBHW082344270726
48658CB00017B/3125